# RAINY DAYS

# HAVING A PARTY

## DENNY ROBSON

## FRANKLIN WATTS
**LONDON · NEW YORK · TORONTO · SYDNEY**

# CONTENTS

*Design:*     David West
               Children's Book Design
*Designer:*   Keith Newell
*Photography:*  Roger Vlitos

© Aladdin Books Ltd 1992

*Created and designed by*
N.W. Books Ltd
28 Percy Street
London W1P 9FF

*First published in*
*Great Britain in 1992 by*
Franklin Watts Ltd
96 Leonard Street
London EC2A 4RH

ISBN 0 7496 0787 4

A CIP catalogue record for this book
is available from the British Library

Printed in Belgium

# Introduction

Most people love parties, whether they are family get-togethers or celebrations with friends for birthdays, Christmas, Hallowe'en or Easter.

You've fixed the date, time and place for your party, so what next? Part of the fun is in getting organised and preparing things in advance so that things go smoothly on the day. You need to decide whether it should be a theme party, like 'Ghouls and Ghosts' at Hallowe'en, what games to play and what food to eat.

This book gives you lots of ideas on how to prepare for your party. There are invitations to make, party hats, fancy dress, ideas for games and even special no-cook cakes that you can make quickly and easily yourself. Have fun!

Here are some of the materials used to make the projects in this book. Most things are not expensive and you may find much of what you need at home. Before you start, gather together everything you need and read the instructions once or twice. It's also a good idea to cover your work surface with newspaper before you start.

# Invitations

Design your party invitations yourself to make them extra special. Here are some ideas for you to try. If you are inviting a lot of people you may want them to be simple, like the balloon invitations, which can be made quickly and easily. If you are having just a few people at your party you can experiment with more elaborate designs.

**You will need**
balloons, tinsel and cotton wool to decorate, card, black paper, red tissue paper, coloured drinking straws, scissors, glue, felt pens.

**1**

**1** First blow up some balloons. Then write the details of your party in felt pen on the sides. You can also decorate them with tinsel and cotton wool if you wish. Let the balloons down and put them in envelopes addressed to your guests.

**2** Draw a picture onto card – a witch or pumpkin for Hallowe'en, or a cracker for a Christmas party. Colour it in, cut it out and write the party details on the back.

**2**

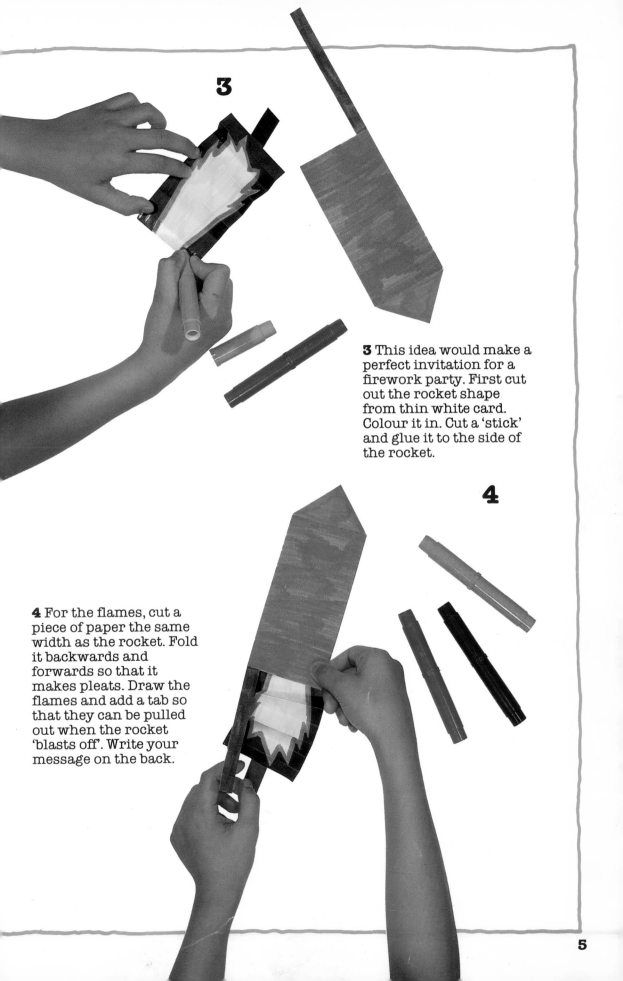

**3** This idea would make a perfect invitation for a firework party. First cut out the rocket shape from thin white card. Colour it in. Cut a 'stick' and glue it to the side of the rocket.

**4** For the flames, cut a piece of paper the same width as the rocket. Fold it backwards and forwards so that it makes pleats. Draw the flames and add a tab so that they can be pulled out when the rocket 'blasts off'. Write your message on the back.

# More invitations

These invitations and their rather special envelopes may take a little more time and skill, but the results are well worth it. Try to think up other designs of your own to make your invitations as original as possible.

**1** This birthday cake envelope contains the burning details of the party! Fold a tab on a rectangle of card and then fold in half. Draw the birthday cake. Cut a strip from the centre of one side and glue red tissue 'jam' behind it as shown. Make cuts in pieces of drinking straws and push them onto the top of the card. Glue the front of the card to the tab.

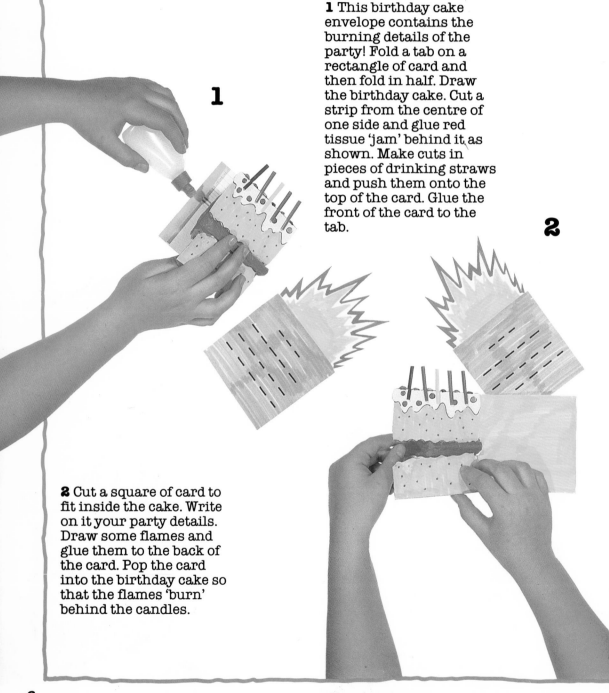

**2** Cut a square of card to fit inside the cake. Write on it your party details. Draw some flames and glue them to the back of the card. Pop the card into the birthday cake so that the flames 'burn' behind the candles.

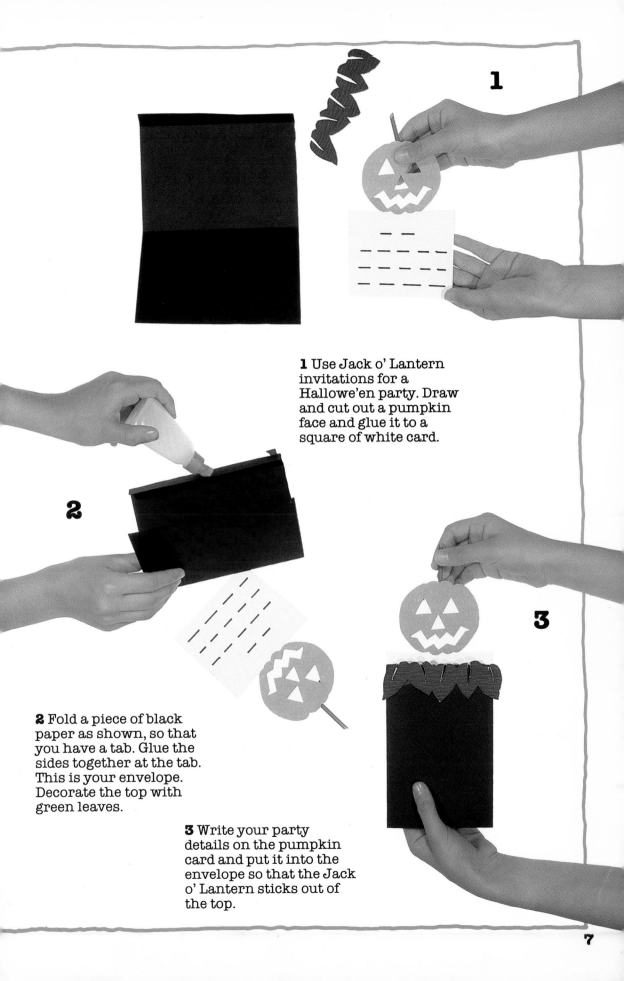

**1** Use Jack o' Lantern invitations for a Hallowe'en party. Draw and cut out a pumpkin face and glue it to a square of white card.

**2** Fold a piece of black paper as shown, so that you have a tab. Glue the sides together at the tab. This is your envelope. Decorate the top with green leaves.

**3** Write your party details on the pumpkin card and put it into the envelope so that the Jack o' Lantern sticks out of the top.

# Party hats

Hats are always fun at parties. To make a very simple hat, cut a strip of tissue paper about 12 cm wide, long enough to fit around the head of the person who is going to wear it, plus a little over to overlap and glue. Fold it into wide pleats, cut out a triangle from the top and glue the ends together. Or you can make more exotic hats, like the fantasy hats on the following pages, guaranteed to make you feel special at your party.

**You will need** white and coloured card, tissue paper, cotton wool, paint, cocktail sticks, silver foil, thread, sticky tape, glue.

### Queen of Hearts
Measure your head with a piece of thread and use this when drawing the outline of the hat. (Remember to add a few centimetres so that you can glue the ends together.) Cover one side with pink tissue. Decorate with a plait of tissue along the bottom of the crown and tissue and cotton wool hearts at the top. Glue or staple the edges together.

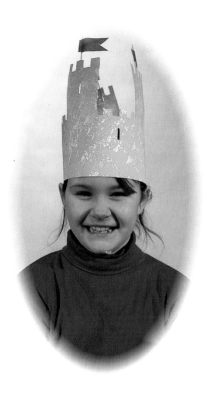

## King of the Castle

**1** Measure your head, draw the outline of the castle with its turrets onto thin card and cut it out.

**2** Paint the castle walls. Instead of using a paint brush, create an unusual effect by dabbing on the paint with cotton wool.

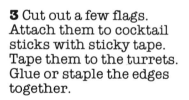

**3** Cut out a few flags. Attach them to cocktail sticks with sticky tape. Tape them to the turrets. Glue or staple the edges together.

## Neptune's Crown

**1** Cut a strip of card to fit your head and cover it with silver foil. Draw the curve-shaped strip onto a piece of card and cut out. Cover with silver foil and glue it to the first strip as shown.

**1**

**2**

**2** Cut out lots of little paper fish. Hang them from the top of the 'waves', using thread and sticky tape.

## Woodland Crown

**1** Measure your head and draw the basic outline of the crown, with its leaves, onto green card. Cut it out. Cut out several thin paper leaves. Use green paper, or paint them different shades of green.

**2** Glue the leaves to the card, add a few strips of coloured tissue for flowers, and glue or staple the edges together.

**1** Fold a square of thin card in half. Draw the face of the rabbit on the bottom half and his ears on the top half of the card. Colour and decorate with cotton wool.

**1**

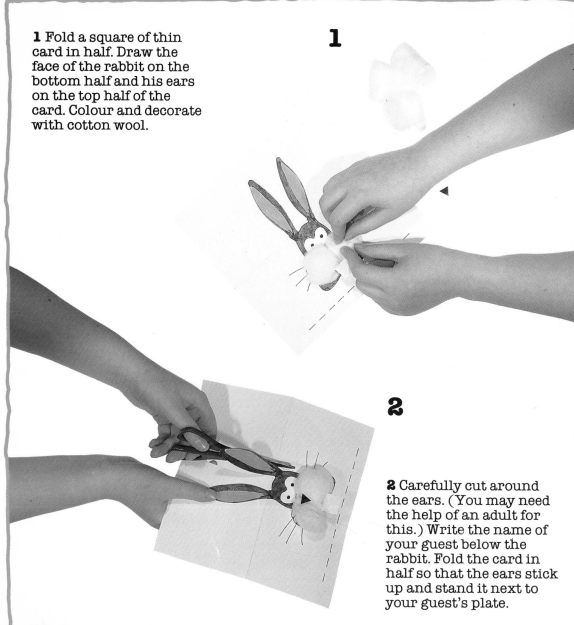

**2**

**2** Carefully cut around the ears. (You may need the help of an adult for this.) Write the name of your guest below the rabbit. Fold the card in half so that the ears stick up and stand it next to your guest's plate.

# Place markers

Many parties involve food and it's a good idea — especially if you have invited lots of people — to make place markers so that everyone knows where to sit. It can avoid a scramble! Make them as simple as you like. Draw faces and names on blank stickers, design a mask to put by each plate, or try these pop-up card ideas.

**You will need**
thin card, felt pens, glue, scissors, cotton wool, tinsel etc to decorate.

**3** For the clown, draw his face below the crease and his hat above. You can use tinsel or wool for hair. Cut around the hat, write your guest's name and fold.

**3**

**4**

**4** You can make lots of different place markers in this way. It can be fun to draw cartoons of your friends' faces and make their hair stick up above the card! Try to think up your own designs.

# Place mats

Make your party table look even more special with these colourful place mats. If the party has a theme, like the circus or an animal party, try to make the place mats fit in with it. If you are making faces, why not turn them into masks by making eye holes and taping string or elastic to the sides. This could even be one of the party games. Get your guests to design their own place mat/mask and give a prize for the best one.

**You will need** thin card, felt pens, poster paints, a small sponge or cotton wool, scissors.

Draw your designs onto thin card, making sure they are bigger than the plates you will use. Cut out and colour them in.

Or you could use stencils to make lots of place mats quite quickly. Design a face for the stencil, like this clown, or draw simple small shapes, like these balloons and presents. Carefully cut out the shapes. Put the stencil on top of the card to be used as the place mat. Dip a sponge or cotton wool into poster paint and then dab it onto the stencil as shown.

# Fancy dress

Getting everyone to dress up can make a party exciting. Fancy dress costumes don't have to be difficult to make or expensive. On the following pages are some ideas for you to try. Other favourites include pirates, gypsies, ghosts, red indians and clowns.

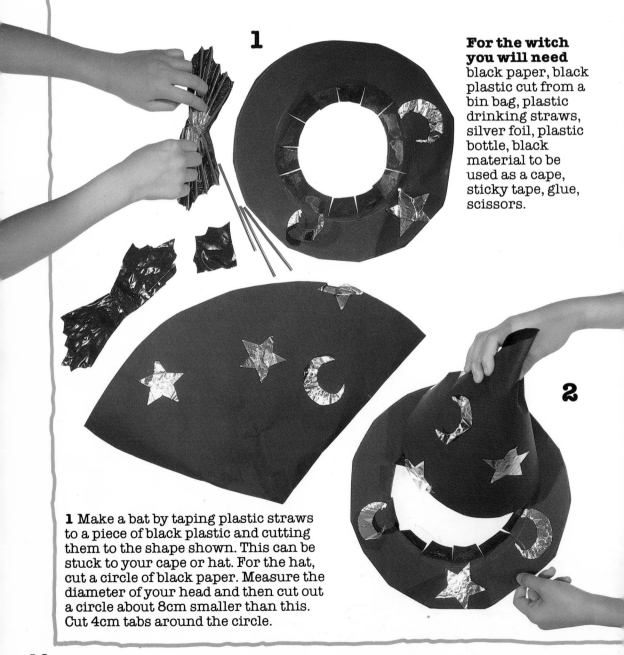

**1**

**For the witch you will need** black paper, black plastic cut from a bin bag, plastic drinking straws, silver foil, plastic bottle, black material to be used as a cape, sticky tape, glue, scissors.

**2**

**1** Make a bat by taping plastic straws to a piece of black plastic and cutting them to the shape shown. This can be stuck to your cape or hat. For the hat, cut a circle of black paper. Measure the diameter of your head and then cut out a circle about 8cm smaller than this. Cut 4cm tabs around the circle.

**2** Cut a fan shape as shown to make the top of the hat. Decorate it with silver foil shapes. Roll it into a cone to fit the brim and glue its edges together. Fold up the tabs on the brim and glue them to the inside of the cone.

**3**

**4**

**3** This creepy spider is simply the bottom cut from a plastic bottle, with eight long black paper legs.

**4** Cover a book with black paper decorated with silver moons and stars for your spell book. Drape yourself with black material, add a few thread 'cobwebs', a little face paint and you're ready for Hallowe'en!

# Skeleton

This skeleton costume is quick, easy and inexpensive to make, but it's very effective — especially at a dimly-lit Hallowe'en party!

**1** Look at the bones of the skeleton laid out on the page opposite. Copy the shapes onto white card, making sure they will fit your body. Cut them out and use black paint or a marker to draw in the spaces between the bones.

**You will need** thin white card, black paint or felt pens, scissors, double-sided sticky tape or safety pins.

1

**2**

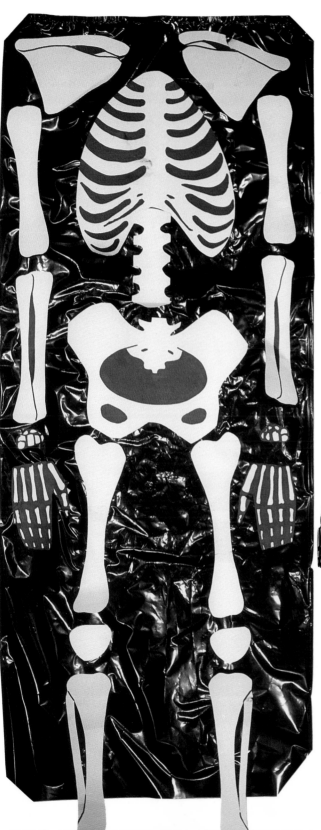

**2** You will need to wear black clothes, gloves and shoes for this costume. Lay out the bones in the correct order and then get a friend or adult to attach the bones to your body with double-sided sticky tape or safety pins. Use white and black face paint for your face and eyes to make the costume appear even more scary.

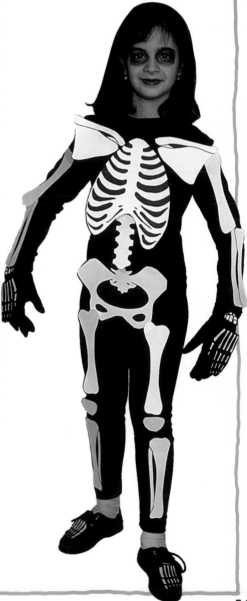

# Bumble bee

This bumble bee costume would make a good fancy dress for a younger child.

**You will need** a strip of black card, two plastic drinking straws, silver foil, thin card for wings, black plastic bin liner, (or a yellow sweater if you have one), yellow card, pencil, felt pens, scissors, double-sided sticky tape, safety pins.

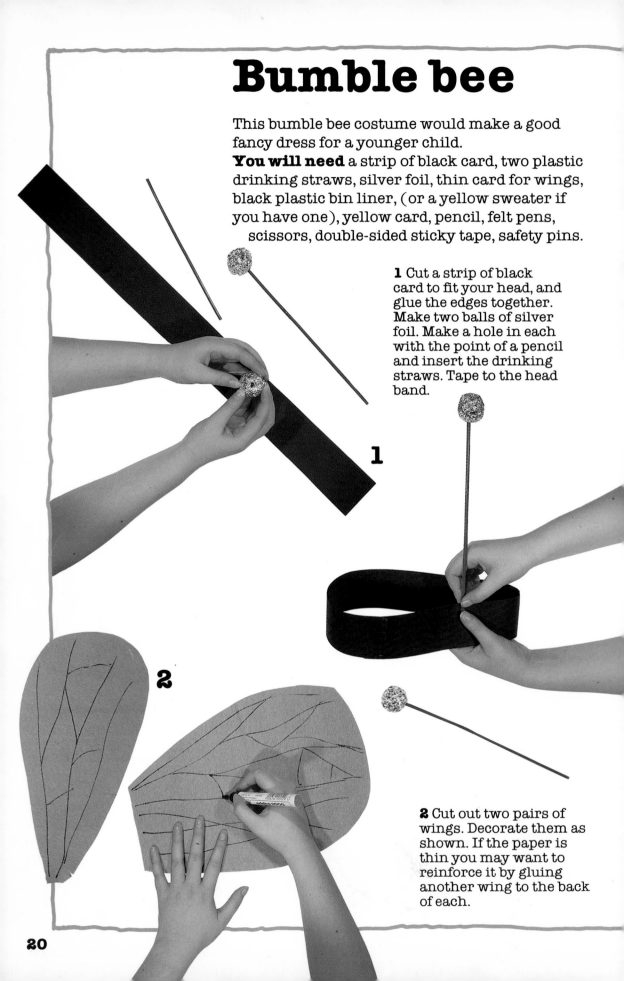

**1** Cut a strip of black card to fit your head, and glue the edges together. Make two balls of silver foil. Make a hole in each with the point of a pencil and insert the drinking straws. Tape to the head band.

**2** Cut out two pairs of wings. Decorate them as shown. If the paper is thin you may want to reinforce it by gluing another wing to the back of each.

**3** Cut neck and arm holes out of a black plastic bin liner. Tear strips of yellow card and tape them to the bin liner. Tape the wings to the other side.

**3**

**4** Carefully put on the bin liner and your antennae. If you have a yellow sweater, you could wear that instead. Pin the wings to the back and decorate the front with black stripes cut from a bin liner.

**4**

**1** Copy the shape on page 32. The dice can be made to any size you like. Draw in the dotted lines and cut along the solid lines. Glue coloured spots on each side, one to six.

# Party games

It's a good idea to plan what games you will play at the party in advance. Make a list, writing down all the things you need for each game. The more games the better, so that you have some in reserve in case you need them. Vary the type of game so that you include musical games, such as musical statues, guessing games, such as memorising items on a tray or guessing tastes, and writing/reading games, such as treasure hunts and consequences.

**To make giant dice, you will need** thin card, pencil, ruler, scissors, coloured paper, glue.

**2** Fold along the dotted lines and unfold. Now fold up into a box shape. Close by tucking in the top flap.

**2**

**The chocolate game**
Everyone loves this game. You need dice, a knife and fork, a plate and a bar of chocolate. Everyone takes turns at throwing the dice. If you get a six, you get to cut off a chunk of chocolate and eat it. For older children, the game can be made more fast and furious. The person who rolls a six must first put on hat, scarf and gloves before trying to cut the chocolate. If someone else gets a six in the meantime, they immediately grab the plate and take over!

# The 'feely' box

This 'feely' box can be used in different ways. You can use it for a memory game. Put lots of different small objects into it, get each guest to feel them and write down as many as they can identify. Or give your guests a Hallowe'en shock by putting a bowl of baked beans or cold spaghetti into the box and then dare them to feel something terrible! You could also use it as a lucky dip to give out take-home presents.

**You will need**
cardboard box, tissue paper, sticky tape, glue, a bin liner, scissors.

**1** Cut a flap in one side of the box. Cut a hole in the lid big enough to comfortably take someone's arm. Tape the lid to the box.

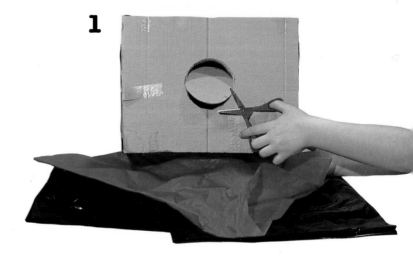

**1**

**2** Decorate the box with tissue paper, securing at the sides with sticky tape.

**2**

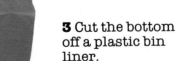

**3** Cut the bottom off a plastic bin liner.

**3**

**4**

**4** Put the bin liner through the hole. Make slits in the bottom of the bin liner and tape to the inside lid of the box.

**5**

**5** Put whatever you like in the box, tape up the flap and you're ready!

**1** To make the papier mâché shell, mix enough flour with water to make a thick, creamy paste. Stand a large balloon in a plastic bowl. Soak newspaper strips in paste and cover the balloon with several layers. When the paper is dry, pop the balloon.

**1**

**2** Paint the shell. Turn it over and glue on paper plate ears, eyes and a nose made from plastic cups, and teeth cut from a paper plate.

**2**

# Sweet monster

This is a good way to end a party and with luck, everyone should get a handful of sweets to go home with. You will need some space for this game. The idea is that everyone takes turns at bashing the monster until it breaks. Then everyone scrambles for the shower of sweets!

**You will need** flour, water, mixing bowl, spoon, strips of newspaper, balloon, plastic bowl, paper plates, plastic cups, crêpe paper, paint, string, sweets.

**3** Give the monster strips of crêpe paper hair and then fill it with sweets.

**3**

**4** Hang the sweet monster in an open space or in a doorway. Get your guests to line up. Give everyone a turn at bashing the monster with a wooden spoon or cardboard roll until the sweets fall out.

**4**

**1** For each colour of icing, sift 50gr (2 oz) of icing sugar into a bowl and add two teaspoons of water or fruit juice. Mix well and add more liquid or icing sugar, depending on the amount and consistency you want. Add one or two drops of food colouring and mix in well.

**2** Pipe a coloured rim around the cake and fill in the centre with white icing. Ice oblong biscuits for feet and teacakes topped with smarties for the bells.

**You will need** a bought round sponge cake, mini swiss roll, teacakes, biscuits, sweets, icing sugar, hot water, food colouring, sieve, mixing bowl, piping bag, (a cone of greaseproof paper will do), jam, spoon.

# Alarm clock cake

Party cakes are fun to prepare. The cakes on the next few pages are easy to make because they don't require cooking. They are decorated with lots of good things to eat, so they are bound to be a success! Try them and then see if you can make up your own cake ideas.

**3** Push finger biscuits into the teacakes and the sponge as shown. Add swiss roll legs and biscuit feet. A touch of jam will help everything to stick.

**3**

**4** Stick 12 square liquorice allsorts around the clock face and a round sweet at the centre. Pipe numbers onto the sweets and add chocolate finger hands to the clock.

**4**

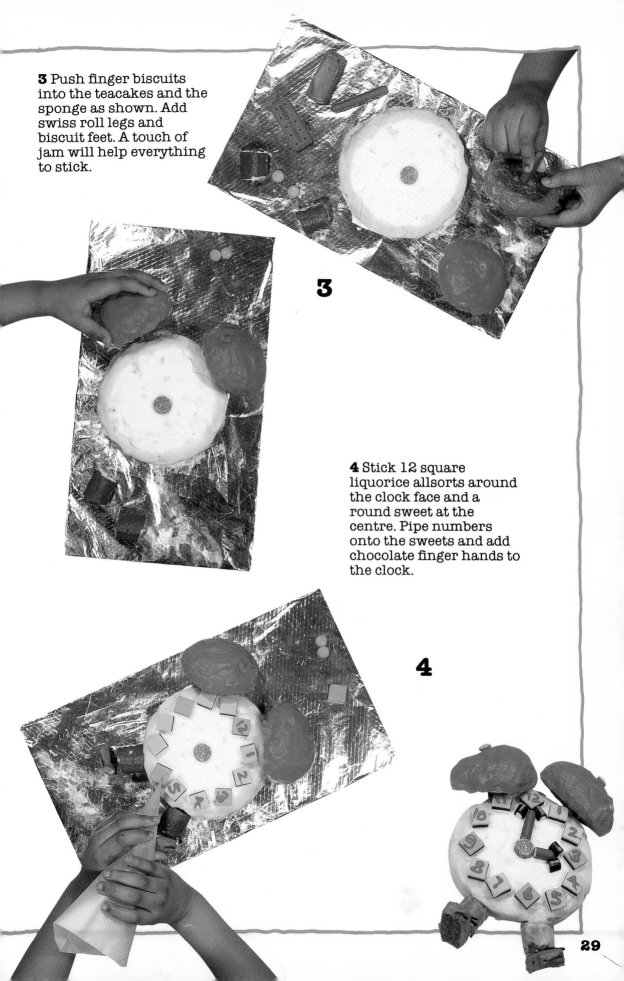

# Caterpillar cake

This is a good cake for younger children. It's easy to make and it doesn't even need to be cut up before you can eat it.

**You will need** a bought swiss roll cake, chocolate finger biscuits, smarties and liquorice allsorts, icing sugar, hot water, food colouring, sieve, mixing bowl, piping bag, jam, spoon.

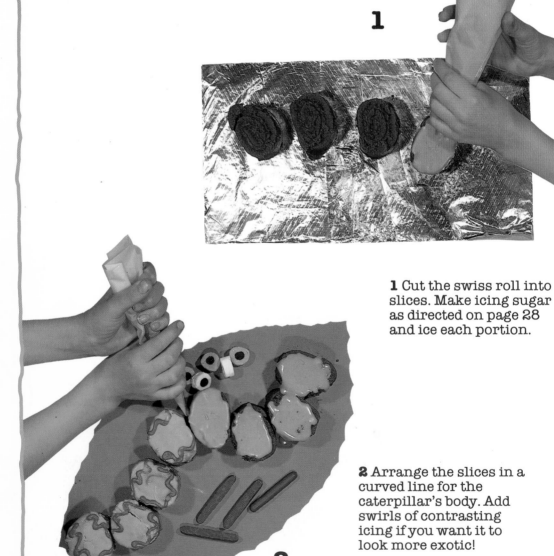

**1**

**1** Cut the swiss roll into slices. Make icing sugar as directed on page 28 and ice each portion.

**2** Arrange the slices in a curved line for the caterpillar's body. Add swirls of contrasting icing if you want it to look more exotic!

**2**

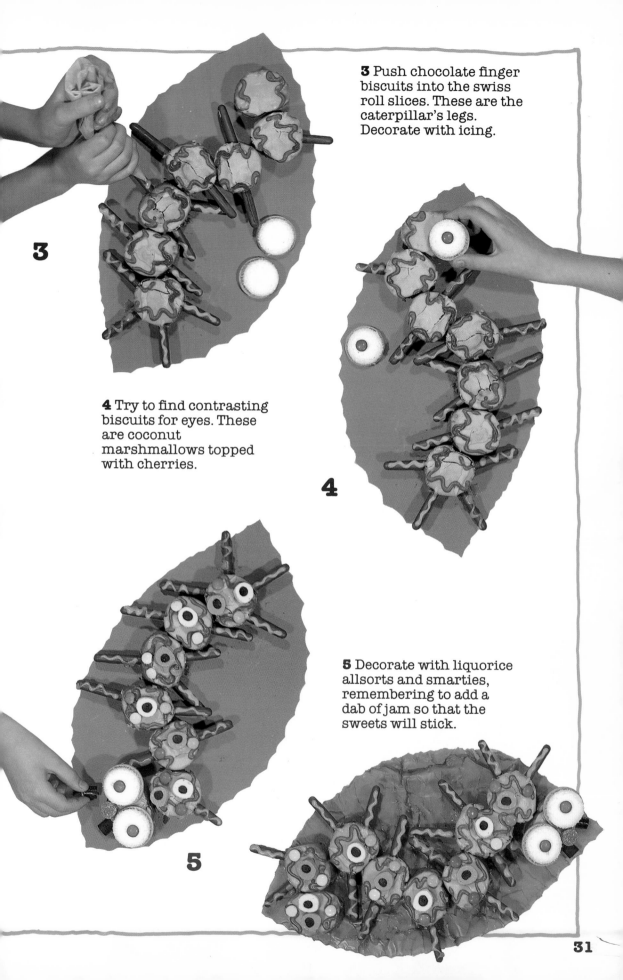

**3** Push chocolate finger biscuits into the swiss roll slices. These are the caterpillar's legs. Decorate with icing.

**3**

**4** Try to find contrasting biscuits for eyes. These are coconut marshmallows topped with cherries.

**4**

**5** Decorate with liquorice allsorts and smarties, remembering to add a dab of jam so that the sweets will stick.

**5**

# Dice design

Copy this design to make the dice shown on page 22. Dice can be made to any size you wish. You could also use the design to make party gift boxes instead of party bags. Fill them with sweets to give to your guests as take-home presents.

# Index